The Lost Pilgrimage Poems

The Lost Pilgrimage Poems

A BOOK OF POETRY BY
JOSEPH D. MILOSCH

Poetic Matrix Press
Madera, CA

Acknowledgements

"Why Is the Scar on a Man..." published by *Poetic Medicine* 1997.
"Mountain Retreat" published by *Magee Park Poets Anthology* Spring1998.
"After Your Long Illness," "Now She Will Bend Away" published by *San Diego Writers' Monthly* March 1999.
"Spanish Enters the Room" published by *Love Is Ageless* 2002.
"Fishing the Day Before My Induction" published by *Magee Park Poetry Anthology* 2001.
"Trip to the Induction Center" published by *Nerve Cowboy* Spring1997.
"I Saw an Incredible Thing" published by *Chiron Review* 2001.
"Flock of Silence" published by *Owen Wister Review* Spring 1996.
"On the Wing" published by *Poems & Plays* 2002.
"A Brief History" accepted for publication by *Afterwards*.
"Grandfather" published by *Poems & Plays* Spring 1997.
"In Memory of My Father's Birthday" published by *Poems & Plays* Spring 1997.
"Burning Black Walnut" published by *Poetry Conspiracy 1996*.
"Woodshedding and Memories of the Engineer's Booth," "Wood Bone Blood" published by *From These Walls* Fall 1996.
"One Night from My Childhood" published by *Tidepools* 2001.
"Staredown" published by *Poems & Plays* Spring 1997.
"Among Men" published by *Poems & Plays* Spring 1997.
"Father Myrick" published by *Tidepools Retrospective* 2000.
"Letters From Paul" published by *Poems & Plays* Spring 1996.
"Latin Met the Anglo-Saxon" published by Tiger's Eye Fall 2005.

Cover Art by Brandon Cesmat

Copyright © 2006 by Joe Milosch

All rights reserved. No part of this book may be used or reproduced in any manner whatsoever without written permission, except in the case of quotes for personal use and brief quotations embodied in critical articles or reviews.

ISBN 0-9714003-8-5

Poetic Matrix Press
PO Box 1223
Madera, CA 93639
www.poeticmatrix.com

To Patsy

CONTENTS

1
"Why is a Scar on a Man..."	9
Mountain Retreat	10
After Your Long Illness	12
Now She Will Bend Away	13
Spanish Enters the Room	14

2
Fishing the Day before My Induction	21
Trip to the Induction Center	23
I Saw an Incredible Thing	25
Flock of Silence	28
On the Wing	31
A Brief History	35

3
Grandfather	39
In Memory of My Father's Birthday	40
Burning Black Walnut	42
Woodshedding the Memories of the Engineer's Booth	45
Wood Bone Blood	48
One Night From My Childhood	50

4
Splitting Wood	55
Staredown	57
Among Men	61
Father Myrick	65
Letters from Paul	69

5
Torn Between the Pull of the World and the Robe	75
Thresholds	76
Latin Met the Anglo-Saxon	80
Meditation at the Church of Our Lady of Guadaloupe, Mexico	82
What Does a Man Do	85
Sixth Meditation at the Crucifix at Our Lady of Guadeloupe Church, Mexico	87

About the Author

Lost Pilgrimage Poems
1

Why Is a Scar on a Man..."

Why is a scar on a man a mark of distinction,
on a woman a mark of disfigurement?

        I don't know.

Why is it funny when a man loses his hair,
and tragic when a woman loses hers?

        I don't know.

Could you make love to a bald headed woman?

What will you tell her
when the X-Rays turn the scar
on her breast raw-
hamburger red?

When she's bald, lost her eyebrows,
and lies closed-eyed
with a skeletal look,
will you kiss her
and tell her
she's beautiful?

        I don't know.

What do you do
in the bedroom,
when she is thinking
of death
and she cries?

        I hold her hand and I breathe.

Mountain Retreat

Four AM too soon.
Waiting for you to wake
I watch three deer,
walking slowly
in a row.

Sun up — moon up.
No distant stars.
Because you are eyebrowless
you wear sunglasses,
refuse to be kissed in lamplight.

I think of the babushka,
covering your bald head
with its azalea
and wood lily pattern.

In a campsite
I can hear a radio.
Someone says,
"Don't touch me
I'm saving myself
for   for..."

We plan to spend
the morning before
your chemotherapy hiking.

Waiting for you, I watch
the wind roll down grass tops,
a rye flow descending the hill
like a kyte's shadow.

Frogs croak in the pond
near the berry bush

as I listen to the tent
door zipper and your footsteps.

You arrive.
We kiss.

Red and yellow
the wildflowers
promise nothing.

After a Long Illness

Your head rests on her stomach.
      Softly she pulls back your hair
in a non-sexual way that is
      sexual. You rub her thigh
in a sexual way that is non-sexual.

There is so much to say that nothing is said
as both of you touch and share.

Now She Will Bend Away

*Timor mortis conturbat me (William Dunbar)**

Now she will bend away to lift
        and shake her skirt. She holds it up
in morning light as if
        she looks for holes
a moth might leave or threads
        loosened by the movement of her hips.

As bees come to the bottle bush
        her song springs in the summer air.
As buzzing breaks my thoughts of death,
        she sings a whispered tune
and shakes her skirt again
        as if it were an offering to
the solstice sun.

        Removing window glaze, I pause
to watch her hanging clothes and rub
        my thumb across my putty knife.
I work as if I have no fear
        I'll leave this world without my dreams,
which seem as rustic
        as the clothes lines bent with weight.

I want to dream that when I die I will
        recall her name. She might be bidding me
a mock farewell, standing alone among
        the lemon shadows of the grass and trees.
I know that corn is cob and stalk,
        and from the mountain's melting ice
come flashing fish.

        She bends away to lift and snap a pillow slip.

*Timor mortis conturbat me (The fear of death confounds me)

Spanish Enters the Room

Spanish enters the room
like a flock of red hooded finches
perching first on TV antennas,
then on the pictures of Cesar Chavez,
family, and the bride and groom
outside the Santa Dominga Church.

In the picture the couple's eyes
are like freshly turned fields
of onion, tomato, and carrot farms,
snug in the county of string ties.

In the kitchen, the women chop ham hocks,
clean cilantro and their conversation takes wing.
Circling above their heads — a sunlit ring —
before it enters the living room, a flock
of red capped finches that perches
among the thickets of Jimmie's ears.

On TV the Forty-Niners run up the score
on the Giants, who are helpless as Jimmie,
sitting in the wheelchair beside me.

Ninety-nine pounds of flesh hides the man
suffering from Alzheimers. He has come to this:
tied to his chair by tape around his wrists;
covered by a rainbow blanket, outlining
the bones protruding from his legs and hips.

Are the women singing a hymn
as they make menudo and beer ices
in the Frigidaire? Whatever they do,
it is for him and the memory of him
eating a late breakfast with a beer
as he watched the game.

Jimmie's eyes are two clumps of soil
kicked aside by the plow in the field
of his past life. In the winter
he pruned apricot and plum trees.
In the summer he picked oranges until
he could no longer remember which side
of the ladder to climb. At those times
he became angry out of fear and pride.

Lorna says, I won't put him in a home.
He won't know anybody. They won't know
his favorite radio station or TV show
or how to make his eggs with a little Tabasco.
There he'll die a hungry, lonely stranger.
Here, he'll die mi esposo.

Lorna enters the living room, ¿Cuanto va San Francisco?
she asks, and waits for the score to flash on the screen.
She rubs his hair as if offering a prayer
that her belief in the after-life will give him a future.

San Francisco is winning, she tells Jimmie,
kissing him lightly
on the ear
and whispering, Que bueno.

She has told me of their life:
She brought him lunch and helped him prune.
Now their life goes beyond the weighing
of words, none of which express
the loneliness of her work or sleep.

As she is about to leave, she tells me
Jimmie was a good worker.
Smart, too.

The look on her face demands shouting,
demands that I see how Jimmie
used both hands at the same time
to pick and bag fruit
without bruising it.

    And if that wasn't possible,

show him walking in his own footsteps
between rows of cotton.

    And if that wasn't possible,

show how the tomatoes he picked became smooth
as identical thoughts in their crate.

    And if that wasn't possible,

let Jimmie do something crazy like dance
a Cebraditas around a warming fire with a pint
and a handkerchief in his hip pocket.

    And if that wasn't possible,

let a crowd of field hands surround
Jimmie in a dance — chanting ritual songs
that celebrate the passing of manhood.

    And if that wasn't possible,

to see the love and respect she carries
in the lines around her eyes.

And if that wasn't possible,
to call Jimmie by his proper name.

And if that wasn't possible,

let Jimmie be himself
before his disease consumed his brain
with snail-like precision.

As Lorna leaves the room,
she leaves in the green plush carpet
only her heel prints to bear witness
to the look in her eyes.

Jimmie faces the screen.
His eyes have not moved all morning.
Sometimes his facial muscles twitch,
making him seem to frown.

We pray that his mind doesn't toil
behind the closed doors of the shed of his body,
that his mind soars like flames on a brush pile,
that under the clouds of his eyes
he wanders fields in November with his breath
seen in the rain as he clips and ties
the finger-thick branches.

He no longer gives signs of recognition or love,
but he lives. He lives somewhere between
the odors of tripe, beef feet, pig feet, hominy,
the announcer's play by play and the smell of coffee perking
through a layer of cinnamon sticks.

He lives surrounded by the sounds of his language,
which are finches riding the air currents,
landing to scratch for food.

Listen!

How their beaks click as they crack small syllabic seeds.

Lost Pilgrimage Poems 2

Fishing the Day before My Induction

for my brother, Mike, who said, be careful.

My brother and I sit silently
in the only friendship we've known. We remain
holding our rods until a sunfish takes his line,
flashes its golden belly and returns
underneath the raft's barrels. In the distance
nothing suggests our friendship won't remain the same.

We have too much on our minds to say
we love each other. We fish in silence
and let our hip's shadows bridge our distance.
Without exchanging glances we remain
looking for the sunfish to return.
Occasionally, we check the rod, bending beneath the line.

Our fate resides in a bean-shaped outline
of a country. Our fear of the future seems the same
as the fear I won't return.
Appearing as golden flashes of silence,
our fears swim in circles and remain
pulling against a thread of diminishing distance.

Looking into the depth, it is hard to fathom distance,
but a hooked worm draws a fish to the line.
Our childhood dreams of heroics remain,
but the excitement for war isn't the same.
Unable to ignore the news, we seek comfort in silence;
as the raft spins on its chain so our fears revolve.

Hooked by our fears of death, we try to return
to the shadows, try to lengthen the distance
from the surface. Eventually, we'll break our silence
like drops of water dripping from our lines.
For now he clowns. Our tongues full of the same
blood he finds on the hook when licking the worm's remains.

Among brothers, childhood memories are remnants
of a ritual where one comrade returns
his catch so the other can receive the same.
We saw the waves breaking in the distance
as we enacted our rituals of hook and line,
defined our friendship and recorded it silently.

As the lake returned our silence, we ignored our lines — our fears
of distance — our guilt, which was the same
for the one who would remain as the one who wished to stay.
                                                    June 1970

Trip to the Induction Center - June 1970

A Father & Son Experience

Driving M-24,
I'm headed to Fort Wayne.
Make no mistake, I'm happy
to leave my hometown.
At 21 I have yet to learn
about the 100 yard stare,
about the fear that rises
from the knowledge
I'm expendable.

Parking,
I walk toward the Fort,
wonder what my dad will say,
hope he won't kiss me
on top of my head
like he did when I was young,
hope he won't shake my hand and cry.

Standing outside the Fort,
we shake hands
as the air between us
grows rock-ribbed with the love
a father sends his son to war.

We look eye to eye.

I try to memorize
the blue of his,
it's shade between sapphire
and the Detroit sky of clouds
streaked with factory smoke
that Saturday in 1970.

Eye to eye, toe to toe,
we shook hands. He gave me words
to soldier by.
And although he didn't speak,
I heard them.

I Saw an Incredible Thing

*Some catastrophes are better than others; with heroin you die slowly,
like a trapper lost in a blizzard..*   *(Dexter) 1971*

The door was open
and I heard a cricket
in the far corner of the tool room.
It was the day after
we passed the general inspection.
In the 187th we
were the only two to pass.
I came to see Dexter
before leaving for two days of leave.

Without permission
he brought his mother
into our tool room,
and Dex stood
his feet together
swinging his arms
like Ed Sullivan,
commanding the attention
of electric cords, sink traps,
saws, rakes, brooms,
and the long handled sledges
grouped in the north corner.

Dexter was higher than I'd ever seen him,
and he took three full minutes to reach
the fittings rack with his hand.
His mother stopped believing
that fashion would continue
after 1962.
She wore a Jackie Kennedy button hat,
a pea green dress, K Mart shoes.
The beads in her necklace
were like her son's teeth,
large, beige,
and loose in their settings.

I saw the thick layers
of her lipstick.
Her eyes blinked
fast,
as if she remembered
an old wives tale
which said blink quickly
eleven times,
pause,
blink faster,
seven times
close your eyes
and the magic will wipe away
the vision of your son's head
falling against wood boxes
and knocking couplings off their ends.

I said,
Dex was the only one
to pass inspection.
She reached out
pushed his hair
back across his temple,
off his wire rimmed glasses.
I saw how
a mother's love
could not heal her son.

Flock Of Silence

Rick and I pulled guard duty on Skunk Hill.
We looked down at two guards
walking among airplanes.
One knelt to tie his boots.
He handed his helmet
to his partner,
who pretended to upchuck in it.

Rick talked about Nam.
How his life was saved
by six blacks
from 'Air Cav.'

Seeing Rick alone,
they could've said,
"His ass is grass."
but they jumped eight feet
from their copters.

They leaped
knowing their heads
could've been minced
by dipping propellers.

They held their positions
when Rick's platoon retreated.
They stood up firing and charged.
They hollered,
as if they were fearless.

The VC stopped,
stared at two copters
that spun like clouds
in the rainy season.

Then the VC wavered,
broke and ran
like dust pushed
by a river of wind.

He showed me pictures of Nam.
He gave me one of himself
in the door of his hootch.

It happens sometimes
when two men are alone at dusk,
one speaks as if the other
cannot hear, the other is a pine,
his ears green fans of needles.
"I was scared, I closed my eyes."

I wonder about the sadness
he wears like the dark scar,
the cuff of our rolled fatigues
leave along floorboards.

His left hand folds into a fist
like he's crumbling a photograph,
and I wonder if he notices the guards
standing in the wing's shade.

"They were black
that's all I know about them."
As he speaks, I see the green
of our helmets, ammo belts,
the camouflaged planes, copters.

Even the concrete runway
appears green
except for the stripe
dividing it in half.

I feel like their rear guard,
though I don't know
what they look like.
That's why he got into it with Riggs,
who didn't want to pull guard duty
with a black man.

Before Nam
Rick would've said forget it,
it's his problem.
Now he doesn't want
to hear that shit.

He feels he has lost his color.
He asks,"Why do I want everything..."
and his voice abandons him
like birds deserting the day
before an indigo flock of silence.

He says,"It's fucking me up,"
as shapes of planes and men
merge in the heat trembling
above the runway.

Ft. Lewis, Washington 1971

On the Wing

I

It was four o'clock on Thanksgiving afternoon and I walked by the creek on my grandparents' farm. The wind blew a light snow across cropless fields, and formed ice webs in grass touching the water. The sun on snow and water warmed the air for a moment before clouds moved between land and sky.

I was looking for something other then a quiet field. I was looking for distance from women with their wine breath, and men boisterous with their whiskey and cigars. Water broke over iced rocks as the clear creek drew me. There were weeds on the bottom. They pulled me with the fascination of mud waves that were V shaped and pointing in the current's direction. It was a sharp tug, a pull the beaver makes as it draws a sapling into its pond. If I could dive, I could swim in a cool world, swim under a wood hut, and surface in a dark dome. There I could breathe odors of bark, wet fur, water.

Earlier I had leaned against the picture window, drawn the frost inside my shirt as I waited for dinner to begin, to end. The T.V. talked about Christmas in Berlin. — What is America going to do to help the Germans?— asked the newsman. "The hell with the Germans!" said my uncle, as he stood up bumping the coffee table. "They should fence off the entire nation. Turn it into a damn concentration camp."

The women raised their chins as if it were important to keep their noses above water. The men backed against the walls or pushed back in their chairs.

Do something Joe, my grandmother told my grandfather. He stood up to my uncle and said, "Let's go to the garage." My uncle went with him. This was not play. My uncle was a paratrooper in the war. Don't give him any more to drink.

If I was one of my uncle's sons and had listened to one his drunken lectures on their laziness, their lack of discipline, how they were never going to amount to shit, I would have gone into the basement and bullied the girls. I am the first born boy among the brothers. My uncle brought me boxing gloves. Brought me ball bats. Took me to see Ted Williams. He called me when the men played pinochle. He showed me his cards, and asked me what to play. Once when I was being punished for a school fight, he visited and told my dad, "Joe, your son has balls, let him go outside."

    It was the war that did it. Butch had such a future, the women were saying, as I followed the men. My grandfather pulled two beers from a bucket behind his tool chest. They stood in the November cold looking at the fields, drinking.

    I stood between them. My uncle placed his hand on my head, and looked down as if he would speak and I would hear all he had to say.

    No one spoke until the wind hit the window and my grandfather put his hand on my shoulder. "Women know nothing of this. They've never been to war."

    "Shit Joe, they've never killed," said my uncle.

    My grandfather said, "You'll go to war and when you return, you'll know." He squeezed my neck and shoulders and pointed to flying ducks above firs along the far field.

    My uncle rubbed the bottle against the winged V tattooed above his wrist.

II

Uncle Butch sat alone
at the kitchen table
looking at his glass,
the table cloth.
Outside snowballs crossed
the roofs of parked cars,
and couples stood on the porch
holding hands and cups

of hot chocolate.

"Is this loneliness
the breaking point?"
were my uncle's words
spoken into a drink.

He had not meant to ruin the day,
but to walk out on the hill in the snow.
He had not meant to talk of his loneliness,
not the loneliness of one in the fields
who knows he has a family
to return to,
the loneliness of a man
sitting at the table
not sure
he is entangled
with his family
the way heat
binds to one
entering from the winter.
He's not sure he loves,
not sure of the next day.
Now the falling snow
would cover the drive,
the walk,
and soon it would be dark.

III

At his grave
twenty years later
I listen to something

I've heard before.

Geese on the wind
honk me home.
Butch, all there is
between us

is
grass,
dirt,
roots.

I went Airborne
to follow you,
and now leave
my wings
on your stone.

A Brief History

We weren't childhood buddies with a history of playing Buffalo Bill
and Sitting Bull. We were two strangers pulling guard duty on
Skunk Hill.

Under a Y-cloud shadow
slivers of water stream
down blades of grass.
They drop on dirt mounds,
foot prints, a gray stone,
soon the season will change.

What if you hadn't enlisted in the Army in '71, hadn't volunteered
for Nam, hadn't hoped a bronze star would transform you into a 100%?

A gopher's head in the den's door,
he is surrounded by five beige birds.
He barks at shadows ringed in sunlight.

And what if we hadn't called you a Cherokee, even though you
corrected us, 'Oglala', if a sergeant from Seattle hadn't disliked you
because you were, quote, "Indian?"

Dropped in the fall, a broad-leaf tree dries.
Its bark, its leaves can't save it.
How much wood keeps a man warm?

Would it have ever been a practical joke?
if you hadn't died, if you'd returned from Nam without a scratch?

I dream of a scarecrow in a corn field.
It's dressed in khaki shirt, army pants.
I see two warriors waving, hear a threadbare hero.

What if you hadn't replaced me at the oversea station?
Would it still have taken 25 years to admit,
I'm a beneficiary of prejudice?

In a season of early scents,
orange and grapefruit blossoms.
I roll over, hold my wife,
count the ohs and ahs of my heart.
Happy to be alive, I feel full
with the urge to cry.

Lost Pilgrimage Poems
3

Grandfather

1900-1992

He talked as if endearing himself to me
was not the reason he taught me to drive,
or taught me how to set a spark plug gap.
I remember the hose under the kitchen porch.
Grandfather's thumb pulled down his bottom lip,
as he rinsed out old chew, and washed his hands.

I drove him past a stump, a burned down barn,
a rusting pump, a gate where black birds perched.
His quick eyes caught pheasants above the corn,
the train's shadow on stalks. He knew the time
required to drive across the tracks and asked,
"Can you beat it?" Then bared his gold-rimmed tooth.

If we could take a ride through Michigan,
his thumbs thumping the steering wheel, he'd talk
about the bridge at Mackinaw, and I
wouldn't dream of light beneath a brass-edged door,
a cricket singing in his fist, and wake
to raise the blind and see a hawk in flight.

In Memory of My Father's Birthday

In the night of the son the earth lies under a black bird with many white dots on its breast and belly.

In the first night of the son
the father arches like a bow
below the window and down the hill
the moon's pointed tip touches
the Maple's January limbs.

In the twelfth year on the night
of the son, my father slept.
His hair fell onto his forehead
and his 5 o'clock shadow spotted his chin.
I watched him sleep
like a father watches his son.
I wanted to brush back his hair.
I didn't because
I was afraid he'd wake,
and we'd both be embarrassed.

In the last year on the night of the son
I didn't know that in five weeks
I'd go to his funeral
or I would have spoken about my love.
I didn't know that our lives would pass
as an iced reflection
of a wood frame house snowbound
behind a stand of two-story pines.
Their frosted needles turned yellow
with the window's lamp light.

On the first anniversary
of the last night
I looked in the mirror,
saw my eyes resembled my father's
with white flecks marking their irises.
When I closed them,
I knew inside his casket the light
was crow-down soft.

Burning Black Walnut

We were snowed in for five days,
when Dad pulled the sled out
to walk into the town store.
As he left he said,
"I'm depending on you,"
then rubbed my head for luck,
opened the door,
and the house sucked in
the outside air
like a deep breath.

While I waited his return,
I listened
to flames gnawing the husks of silence.
It was dark.
I looked at our crystal lampshade
bright with reflected fire,
our mantle holding Dad's tobacco can,
pipe rack and our black phone.
I ran my hands
over the red brick fireplace,
over the tips of smoke stains
sharpened like points
of log walls in a frontier fort.
I wondered if Dad remembered
to dodge the weak ice
that snaked around island shorelines.
I went to the window,
pressed my eyebrow to the glass
and crossed myself
in a quiet prayer.
Outside, clouds slipped under stars
as the evergreens stretched
against our storm windows.

Something was wrong.
Mom was not talking
as she wrapped me in a blanket.
I complained it scratched my neck.
She snapped, "Stop whining
like a girl,"
then rapped me on the head
with her finger.
That was before
Dad returned that night
with frost caked to the collar
of his navy peacoat,
around the flaps
of his plaid cap.
He stood as if sculptured
out of iced air.
He gathered scrap lumber
from the basement.
He pulled nails
out of the 6 X 8 inch
pine boards, cut them
along with two-by-fours
and the old window frame
he found beside
two chunks of coal.
He burned everything
including the black walnut
he was saving for a coffee table.

Today the March wind runs
its fingers thick with the smell
of rain through my hair.
Dad, I miss your cold fingers
rubbing my hair that December day.
I try to remember
the smell of your breath,
the warmth of your hands,
your footsteps
coming down the stairs.
I want to face the wind
with more than a memory
of myself wrapped in a blanket
near the fire when it was winter.
By the staircase
the floor lamp's shadow
took the shape of a cupped hand,
rising above the linoleum.

Woodshedding and Memories of the Engineer's Booth

for Louie Armstrong and the Blind Boys

The wind twisted his hair as Joseph stood
looking across the ruins of his childhood home:
wheel ruts leading to a corncrib,
a course of bricks under a layer of sod.
        Three robins flew above these mounds,
        sprinkled with weeds and spaces of absence.

Time's blue-collar hands broke this place,
and sunlight trimmed the walnut's shade
as well as shade from warping boards,
a sagging roof and a doorless shed.
        The trio cupped the wind and lowered their legs
        above the gentle mist, the broken bricks.

The shed's floor held a scatter of bolts,
a metal band, and fungus coated leaves.
He could not wait to master music
and practice took him somewhere else.
        The red breasts settled by a twist of brush
        as a cricket leapt from well to ground.

His talent for singing Polish hymns
and mimicking a gospel tenor earned him
his clarinet and gave him dreams
of leaving his loneliness.
        A chipmunk paused to listen for
        the slightest puff by owl or cat.

Woodshedding with his horn,
he spent hours battling his woodwind.
Surrendering, it opened a path
worn by a reedy breath.
> Wind eddied among the boards grown old,
> an otter looking for the marsh it smells.

He learned to love his clarinet
the night he heard Goodman play.
Spellbound and drawn down a long
tunnel of sound, he refused to dance.
> Oil stains sprinkled the floor under the shade
> of barley sprouts, stooping with withered corns.

The night he worked with Louie he learned
to hear what he read, enabling him to feel music.
His ears didn't explode with shooting stars,
but he entered the world of paper, of ink.
> Under this ragged roof, the walls held notes,
> and wind was powerless to free them.

Memories of Louie loosening his new tie,
uncuffing his freshly cleaned
and freshly pressed shirt walked arm in arm
with an old dream across the cracked earthen floor.
Joseph remembered how long it took him
to learn the scales and to keep time,
how take after take he tapped his toes
against the clarinet case
resting between his feet.
> He remained patient waiting
> — waiting —
> for the chance to be heard.

Absently tapping his toe against a trio of rocks,
Joseph snapped his fingers in 2/4 time. He didn't smile
or cry, but it seemed the nakedness of his anguish
could never be buried in a field or under a stone.
      He mourned this place, humming a tune
      with shadows visible to hanging bats.

Wood   Bone   Blood

for Steven Hawk

Dragging my palm along the table's edge,
I slide my hand against the grain.

A sliver breaks beneath my skin.
"What have you learned from your mistake?"

Look at the damage you've done by
moving before you think,"
Dad points out a crack
wide as a sunfish bone.

"Never go against the grain," he says,
taking a needle from the cloth
he'd stapled to his bench.

He strikes a match, begins to tell
about the buck he found three days dead
with its lower jaw shot off.

I want to shut my eyes and hide my fear,
but my eyes are held in the tender gaze
of his finger's shadow.

I watch him heat the needles' point, "Don't jerk,"
he says before he pricks my hand.
The trick is trusting his touch.

Focused on my hand he talks
of that starved deer,
its tongue touching the grass.

He says, "If you wound an animal,
track it, find it,
put it out of its misery."

Finding the sliver's tip, he pulls it.
I bleed. He says, "Lick it,
a little pain never hurts."

Replacing his needle, he returns
to his work, his shadow
sliding across the table.

The scratch of sandpaper
bears witness to the even grain.
A bead of my blood grows.

One Night from My Childhood

for my father

*"Consume my heart away; sick with desire
And fastened to a dying animal."*
(W.B. Yeats)

Your clarinet
lies sleeping
in the case lined
with purple velvet,
the color of cloth
covering statues
during Lent.

At night your clarinet
calls me in mid-sleep.
It touches me
with a touch
as soft as a b flat.

I rock your clarinet
through the night.
I read to it
a few lines from
"Sailing to Byzantium."

Why didn't I inherit
your lips, your lungs,
your throat swelling with air?

Your clarinet thinks,
Yeats is a
poor substitute
for you
even while I
place my lips
close to its reed,
whispering verses.

We spend
our slow nights together,
holding our memories
within ourselves.

As for my soul,
it has forgotten everything
except one night
from my childhood
in Hamtramck.
For three hours,
you practiced playing
the same notes,
softly
over and over
as I slept
on the couch
between flat pillows.

Lost Pilgrimage Poems
4

Splitting Wood

For the Czech widow, Mrs. Kravoc

Her husband died and would appear at dusk
attracted by the sounds of steel in wood.
A lumberjack he came the way of storms
and left her clues: a clump of muddy snow,
a dust of salt on tablecloth.

                She swore
he wore a pair of rubber boots, and swirled
his leather gloves around his working cap.
These days a handy man is hard to find
who can afford to work for what I'll pay.

She lived under her dusky, cotton shawl
among odors of smoke, ham hocks, and beans.
These odors followed her. They seeped from strands
of braids, her skirt, as rows of vegetables
unfurled beneath her skin.

                Her house of brick
and wood built into a hill and divided
in two. The upper floor – a paradise
of China, wood, and lace – was rarely seen
and held a special sadness for the weekly hour
of melancholy dreams: the guild or priest
for tea and prayer in rooms with clear lake air.

The downstairs hid a fairy ring of sights:
a crate of herbs, a box of Lucky Strikes,
and burls of socks connected purple balls
on slippers by the hide-away.

                She taught
me how to split the log by setting it
on end, and looking for its spot. The place
the grain signed to the eye it would accept,
or maybe more, it would invite the axe.

I learned the proper place of myth and stories
in accepting the curious mix of ache
with happiness. To speak or chant a tale:
beneath the snow the working ant is safe;
helps lift the gloom of thaw and freeze in spring
or fall when axe will shiver through hands and arms
to stitch the log to bone.

                Unknowingly, we lived
on common ground of young and old, a place
the axe, the wedge, the mallet breathed like beams
of lantern light where will and muscle met.

She taught me to accept the pain and joke
about her splitting more at 65 than I at 17.
After we chopped and stacked a cord,
we'd brush off snow and sit
inside amid the smell of barley soup.
She'd pour a cup of tea and serve corn bread
or jelly rolls, or chips.

                As from the couch,
I listened to her as she stirred her drink,
or whittled bears, or boats, or checked
a pot of soup simmering on the stove
where beef and bones were weighted and balanced like logs
in stories where the work had mortal stakes.

Staredown

> *"Hitting is a battle like a boxing match."*
> JM (Sr.) 1960

My father kicked the mound's dirt.
His face, behind a half mask
of shadows, dripped sweat.
He preached, "Stare down the pitcher,
intimidate him."
He hollered from the mound,
"Look me in the eyes
when I'm pitching to you."
We knew he threw his fastball overhand,
his curve sidearm. We both knew
I couldn't stare him down
and pick up his arm in time
to adjust to his pitch.
We were learning about rivalry.
How competition is concealed
in advice the way a pitcher
hides his grip with his glove.

Stepping out of the box,
I looked at mulberry leaves
growing as thick as ivy
over the outfield fence.
I wanted to wear sunglasses
to escape his eyes.
"Sunglasses are for hoods."
It was like after church,
when the Statwick girls
made a point of talking
to Mike and me.
On the way home dad said,
"Joe Dimaggio wouldn't have made it
to first base with Marilyn
if he hadn't been a star."

"Afraid I'll stick it in your ear,"
Dad yelled from the mound.
My brother Mike loved it.
He called, "Bunt! Bunt!
You're not looking at his eyes."
Mike was o.k., we were both
in love with Jackie Kennedy.
We believed our politics
came from our hearts.
"How could anyone vote for Nixon?
His wife is uglier than he is."
We liked JFK.
Jackie made us believe
there was magic in a woman's kiss.
We thought her kisses
would be as unique as mulberries.
The girls we knew
would be like their mothers;
tie rags around the curlers
in their hair, shop
in open toe shoes with chipped
nail polish and dirt
around their toe nails.
For a woman like Jackie,
we'd have to go to some exotic place
like Massachusetts or Annapolis.

Years later Mike and I watched
geese land near marshes
at the Pine's south end.
He said, "If I had a gun,
I could shoot the lead one's beak off,
a little chin music."
For us it was the worst time of year
too warm to play hockey,
too cold for baseball.
It was the time of year when the trees
surrendered to the color brown,
the water looked brown,
as it washed over beach sand,
the cut corn stalks became spikes
in the fields, and stacked hay
became a crow's perch.
The day JFK was killed
we were sent home and our lives
became a barren infield
as we watched Jackie
pulling John into her lap.
We saw her face. We saw
that girls could learn terror
in the back seat
of an open convertible.

Later, we dreamed of capturing
the photographer who followed
Jackie everywhere. We wanted
to shove his camera down his throat
like we wanted to drive
our Dad's fastball up the box,
tearing the pitcher's head off.
The same summer we cut photos
of Jackie and kept them in our shoe box
next to cards of Mantle, Maris,
Musial, and Mudcat Grant.
The same summer the only pain
we dealt with was the pain
of a fastball across our knuckles
on a blown bunt attempt.
The same year the mulberry trees
outside the left field fence
became more reachable
than the moon.

Among Men

I

My Grandfather said,
    "Poles can cry and polka at the same time,
    if they don't trade their honor for money."
My uncles said,
    "Poles can cry and dance at the same time."
My cousins say,
    "Men don't cry.

I am in the July morning
watching the brood of quail
marching from behind the wood pile.
See the cock. Its head bobs side to side.
Smell the heat, hot grasses.
Patsy and I hold each other
after we cried
the night before her lumpectomy.

Now we kiss and our breath
holds hands, dancing
to the fear of cancer,
dancing to our blood beat.

At work I'm replaced
by a younger man. A single man
without problems.
Patsy worries about my job.
I tell her, "I was looking for a job
when I found this one."

II

My grandfather said,
    "God makes you rich, and He gives
    the rich responsibilities for the poor."
My uncles said,
    "With money comes responsibilities."
My cousins say,
    "There will always be poor."

My wife lies in bed draining fluid
from her operation
through a plastic tube
into a plastic bottle.
I empty the bottle, smell old caked socks.
Patsy says, "I'm glad we're not poor."
I don't tell her at work the secretary
pulled me aside told me it was
in my best interest to use Patsy's health
insurance. That is, if I wanted
to continue to work for this company.
Nothing personal, the boss
doesn't want higher insurance rates.

III

My grandfather said,
> "Any man who cheats on his wife will cheat in
> business."

My uncles said,
> "If you are going to cheat on your wife
> don't do it in the town where you live."

My cousins say,
> "A real man takes a woman every chance he gets."

The blade hand, who taught me my trade
in the dirt, told Patsy,
"Joe's a throw back to when
a man's word meant something."

> Step lightly now, be careful
> of the toes,
> whose shadow wears
> a wormwood suit.

I know I'm as much a part of my cousins
as I am my uncles and grandfather.

I know when I tell my wife I love her,
I use such a small portion of my throat.

I know if I could tell my wife I love her,
using my entire throat, I could speak words to live by.

All these thoughts twist,
right now,
around my maleness
like mistletoe in a sycamore.

Soon my leaves will fall
and my limbs will feel lighter than air.

Soon my bark will flake
in fist-size ovals.

Soon it will be morning
and the aroma of coffee
will carry the odor of leaf litter and fog.

Father Myrick

When I was in Catholic school
in the seventh grade, our school
was next to our church.
The church shaped
like a cross and built out of
quarry rocks gathered by the parish men.
The pastor, a chaplain in the second
world war, was trapped
behind enemy lines without a weapon.
"I made it by
the grace of God," he said
in an Irish brogue and
never discussed any more of the battles
he experienced in North Africa,
the heel of Italy, and outside Rome.

As boys, we compared him
to a Rocky Marciano version
of Friar Tuck. We would look
at the lines of his body,
the symmetrical twin of
the maple. We believed he was made
of concrete, asphalt, and the hardwood
found in the sculpture,
supporting the church altar.

When I was in Catholic school
in the seventh grade,
my favorite time was winter.
Especially, the times it snowed.
From my window seat,
I could see a cove downhill
past the rectory. An island
of marsh reeds grew in the middle
of the pond. A maple stood there
with four leaves blinking like the
constellation Pegasus.
Surrounded by thorn bushes,
it became a mystical castle
appearing and disappearing
behind a curtain of snow.

The wind warped trees and
the shadow-skating clouds were a view
forbidden by the nuns as evening TV
was forbidden by my parents.

Sometimes, I could see Father
in his long black overcoat, walking
the bank. At these times, I thought
if I could look into his eyes,
I would learn the truth about war.

So secretly the solitary figure
walked through the landscape.
His footsteps cracked echoes
and he paced as if he was naked
under his shadow that he wore
like the robe of a twelfth
century monk. It hid his true
identity just as the monk's
robe hid King Richard
the Lion Hearted
in the TV show Robin Hood.

In the seventh grade the winter
seemed particularly harsh.
So cold that half the class
would stay inside
during recess. Only the hardy
would brave the cold.
Sometimes a few would choose
to face the cold and escape
the eyes of the nuns,
who would only see burnt
swastikas in the fantasies
of a young man.

On a day of wind whipped snow,
I went solo, creeping beyond
the nuns' boundary to gain
a clear look at that maple. I told
my buddies, "I am a knight errant
in search of the Holy Grail," and left them
safe in the parking lot
and went for the clear shot
at that frosty-bearded tree.

I was looking for adventure
when the pastor caught me
stealing wine from the sacristy.
He took me into his rectory,
poured me a shot of Irish Whiskey,
told me men drink openly.
Men didn't steal their alcohol.

Then he sent me, I'm sure,
reeking of whiskey
into Mother Herman's class.
I sat as she read a child's version
of Hamlet and my head spun
like a blizzard
over the playground.

Letters from Paul

I

You write, "I don't know how I came to be there, or how I was able to
get out. Released from Chino in April. The rains came hard."

As I worked cutting slopes,
building house pads, streets, or swales,
I would lift my head, look at the foothills
and think how freely wild barley turns.

Think how easily I go to my truck in the morning
with my coffee, my cap, and my keys.
My lunch box holds apples, cucumbers,
sausage sandwiches, and a short chili.
How easy I collect my tools and drive.

About the rains, how can I express my pleasure
in the sawed lumber rain smell of my garage?
How can I express the feelings of my hands
when they grip solid wood and hard steel tools?

II

"Last night I woke at 4 a.m.. I was in Motel 6 and the rooms seemed so big, so light, so uncramped. I pulled the curtain open and sat drinking ice water watching the early morning traffic. People with somewhere to go."

At the window
in the county jail
overlooking the bay
a first timer
wearing cuffs
around ankles,
wrists, has eyes
of a sand shark.
He touches
his reflection,
again
he noses the glass.

III

"To tell you some men were regularly abused. They had the face of
a woman tattooed on their backs. Now those words have the
same meaning to me as my first letter to you when I wrote,
`Everything
is for a very short time.'"

Rounded points
plant black roses
in the arms
of the Market Street people.
Dust cakes
the fronts of their teeth,
and puta marks
cross their names.
Prison tattoos
are on the arm and back
of the un-manned one.
If only
he could forget
the nights
of his sentence.
Forget nights
his body
was for other men,
and his spirit
had its neck bones
thrust
through the meat of its neck.
His shirt hides
the blue faced woman.
She smiles from his back,
gives him the name

Otra Hombre.
Now his finger
touches the dark bud,
whose roots spread
in his veins,
whose nectar
surfaces
as the glaze
over his eyes.
It takes away
the fright
of mirrored reflections,
and dims the gaze
of other men.

Lost Pilgrimage Poems
5

Torn Between the Pull of the World and the Robe

Torn between the pull of the world and the robe,
I talked to Father Otto, the prefect of Noel Hall.
He said, "Read St. Jerome and John Clare."

I read before evening prayers, and afterwards
I walked the harvested cornfields. This is how
the Holy Days of October transitioned into November.

I was among those who dreamt of sainthood or writing
or preaching. John Clare gave me strange dreams of dancing
like the mythical children known as the Pleiades.

Like them I was attracted to dance and to
ignore my parents' call. I wished to be like them,
an immortal and distant constellation.

I played chess with those who discussed
whether it was better to be visited by the God
of Abraham or the God of Moses.

The argument — it is better for God to come
for dinner and stay for drinks than it is to be
felled from fear — seemed glib.

Occasionally I found solace in the saints but most often
I found it in Joyce or found it by walking through
ploughed fields, proging clumps of roots and dirt.

Still, I was unprepared for the coming of winter.
The stars shrank as a wedge of cold air drove between us.
Then, the solstice brought small drifts of snow
to bridge the fields' furrows.

Thresholds

I

During my year at Saint Joe's, a miserable fear
about losing my faith surfaced. I thought
a woman could never love a faithless man.
In the year of confusion, it was a bleak time:
larva slept beneath the maple's bark
and the cry-crawl sound of cloth
scurried across pews.

Longing for an impeccable quiet, I sat
in a remote pew, thinking about ice,
the heat of salt and snow covered fields
where moonlight appeared brittle.

Should I've cried over my loss
like a father sobbing at his child's funeral?

II

According to Father Martin, Divine Guidance
was the inspiration to cut a lunch bag
and use it to cover Joyce's Dubliners.
Inspiration drew the cross in the middle
of the cover, drew the circle
circumscribing the cross; and wrote
The Lives of the Saints around its circumference.

During evening prayers, I sat reading and thinking
about meditating or the end of one story
or the beginning of the next.

I was like ice by the time I learned
about the heat of salt. There were holes
burned into me, and wind, fresh
from crossing fields of winter wheat,
blew through me, making a faraway sigh.

III

During the winter solstice,
I looped a rosary
around my fingers as I waited
for the appearance from deep inside me
of the one who could sit easily with himself,
who could take comfort from the pictures,
the statues, and the silence.
In the hour of knowing, ideas took on
the pure smell of the body,
and genuflecting,
I received a vision:
the chapel with its smells
of incense and candles
encouraged death to rise refreshed
as trees cracked and sap shivered.

IV

Of course, it was obvious,
to live a life one had to cross
then re-cross the threshold.

As I stepped outside the church,
the night was cloudless.
Snow fell from the eaves
and swirled with the wind
as if it knew,
a man dying without faith
attended the marriage of two deaths.

V

Ice loaded branches clicked upon themselves
as I walked with Joyce in my pocket.
I thought of winter parties,
of skate-dancing,
of bodies exchanging their warmth
through the gloved connection
of the palms. Thought of a bluebell
on the toe of Nancy's skate,
candy kisses,
and moonlight catching
a lipstick stain
on hot chocolate's cup.

How could I imagine
returning to earth?

Latin Met the Anglo-Saxon

In Latin class we were bored.
In the hallways we'd say, Carl sed est.
We translated it loosely to mean Carl's an ass.

We'd change phrases we were to memorize
from nil sine Numine
(nothing without Providence)
to nil sine nivibus
(nothing without snow).
We'd call new students
testibus torpidus
(numb nuts).

We thought the priests didn't have a clue,
but our wit was our discovery of clichés
known since Latin mingled with the Anglo-Saxon.

It was tradition renewed through the ritual
of meditation and study. Forty years later,
a few phrases of nonsense are the remnants
of mornings when I walked under trees, reciting
conjugations and noticing nothing but shadows.

Language veiled the mystery of loss and gain
the same way women hinted at their hidden magic
when they danced in the halls of Chicago,
which we called Urbs Ventosa — the Windy City.

I remember how my eyes would glaze over
when I received an A on a translation
or when I received an unexpected glance
from a woman in a tight skirt. What happened
to the excitement at sighting a glimpse of the mystery?

Ubi tete occultabas! I call out, "Where have you been hiding?"
I can't find you in the smell of the harvested hay
or coffee on a wintry morning. Entering the month
following the Harvest Moon, I walk Holy Jim Trail.
Sitting on a rock, I watch the wind herd clouds into a clover.
Above the distant ocean a stray cloud worms westward,
and the sun transforms the thin and opaque vapor
into orange and raw sienna. The air stops and seems
to wait for quail to burst from brush like faith.

Meditation at the Church of Our Lady of Guadeloupe, Mexico

for minerva

I
The Benedictines built the rock wall surrounding their monastery.
It was five feet tall. Each rock picked from the roadside in spring. Each rock culled for its regular shape and its shade of brown, gray,
or gold.

Father Martin used it as an example of celebrating God through work. A graying man, his eyes were horned-shaped rays darkened
by his tan and enlarged by his wire rimmed glasses. Fall was his favorite time of year. As the rocks warmed in the sun and cooled in the shade, he would become philosophical. Pointing to the wall,
he'd say, "Faith is like those rocks, it heats up — cools — and grows warm again."

Other times he spoke from his heart. Celibacy is a superficial argument. Of course men like woman. God made it so. Don't use women as your excuse not to become a priest, or blame them for your loss of faith. If you need proof of God's existence, watch a sunset. None of God's other creature's can appreciate a sunset — not birds, dogs or horses. Cats don't admire a bird's feathers — they don't wear them in their fur. God only lets man see beauty because it's God's way of revealing himself. Mark my words. Everything is beautiful because beauty is God, and he's in everything.

    The Mississippi south of Saint Louis.
        The Sault Saint Marie in October.
The Grand Canyon from a tent
    along the banks of the Colorado.
Santa Fe. Niagara Falls. Puebla, Mexico.

    Coyotes standing in the shade of a Surgarro.
Quails pecking through oak leaves.
    Red tail hawks. Golden eagles. Gray whales
blowing off the coast of Baja.

Sometimes holding a handful of duff,
    I watch a spider crawl from the rubble
and wonder why I don't feel God's presence.
    Sometimes, I wonder if I ever felt him.

    Once maybe in December.
        After confession.
    On the steps of St. Joseph's.
        At twelve or thirteen.
Two feet of fresh snow had fallen.
    A light snow continued.
Mother came outside.
    The street light lit up her hair.
She placed a gloved hand on my shoulder.
    Kissed me on the forehead.
Her breath smelled of Certs.
    A light snow continued to fall.

II

       Confined as I am between the bricks
and bones of my church and head,
       it is hard to feel comfort;
and faith is always on the other side
       of stained glass windows, carved doors,
and the crucifix with blood dripping
       from the toes of the Son.

Sometimes I become fearful
       when I believe I'll rot alone in my grave.
Sometimes I'm anxious of my body
       testifying against me
when I'm alone with God.
       Always I'm half and half,
knowing the light of stars passes through me,
       and heaven is full of saints.

What Does A Man Do

As a young man in the seminary, Father Martin asked
us to meditate on this question, "What does a man do
when he's alone with his aloneness?" At seventeen I felt
so alone I was embarrassed to say what I would do.
Because I couldn't sleep, I walked through the maples
every morning between 3:30 and 5. I touched the moss,
growing on the damp side of trees. I watched the sun
lightening the sky by outlining clouds and hoped
for a sudden appearance of thunderheads.

At seventeen my loneliness followed me
wearing its veil of blades. The gardener,
who I passed on the way to class, seemed
content as he nurtured the pruned plants
and vines until they became immersed
in their colors. I thought of him as
a sentry standing on the rim of rebirth.

One time a storm came from different bearings
at once. Hail flew from the four cardinal
directions and the storm thrust the edges
of its wind against my eyes.
In the chapel I read the Sacred Mysteries
of Our Lord's Passion and Death. I tried
not to think or believe — those who die faithless
would be left without sanctified graves, without keepers,
and their bones would be swept by the wind.

Now during my morning meditations,
I enjoy the smell of my garden and lawn.
When I harvest my tomatoes or weeds,
I'm tempted to taste the soil, keeping fresh
my memory of feeling afraid of myself.

A fear generated during the time my body
wouldn't let my mind rest or enjoy the vocaling
of canticles or psalms. My only choice was to lie
among the green candles burning in the grass
and eavesdrop on the distant laughter of others
on their way to prayers, as I listened,
I never lost sight of what occurred in the hours
of shadows and cold air, when an owl pruned,
called out, and tossed bone pellets made inside itself.

Sixth Meditation at the Crucifix at Our Lady of Guadeloupe Church, Mexico

      With extreme precision,
the sculptor formed
      into volcano cones
the flaps of skin encircling the knees.
      He covered the exposed bones
with a splash of paint
      and ran a wedge of red
down the shins to the toes of Christ.

I

Señor. Señor.
Whispered the man kissing his fingers
before touching the knees of the crucified Christ.

Señor. Señor.
He spoke before kissing his fingers
worn smooth by concrete and block.

Touching the worn knees of the crucified,
the man spoke as if addressing
his father or uncle.

Señor. Señor.
      Papa. Papa.
Tio. Tio.
      Señor. Señor.

And the blood dripping sculpture
looked at the man who tugged the top
of his worn at the knees pants.

II

        The man wraps his rosary
around his knuckles like a bandage.
        He reminds me of my grandfather,
who gave me my first suit.
        A brown tweed with a matching,
five button down vest. He said,
        "I bought this when I was thirty-three
and thought I'd be buried in it,
        but now I'm too fat, and you've grown into it."
This tweed was a remnant from the time
        when men would buy
and wear to church the clothes
        they'd be buried in.
By the time of their funeral,
        they became comfortable
in the suit they'd wear for eternity.

III

Two men with a fistful of beads
know if the statue would blink,
cry, spit, it would awaken in them
the truth of who they are,
but the night sometimes forgets
its moon and morning star.

After kissing his fingers,
they become as gentle
as the shadow of a dove
flying in the belfry.
Then, he touches the knees of Christ.

Pocketing my rosary,
I wonder if I can achieve more
than a pantomime of faith?

About the Author

Joe Milosch graduated in 1995 with his MFA from San Diego State University. He has published poetry and essays in various magazines over the past ten years. His first chapbook, *On the Wing*, was published by Barnes and Noble as a regional publication; his second chapbook *Father of Boards and Woodwinds*, was published by Inevitable Press for the Launa Poets Series. He was a finalist in the Tennessee Middle State Chapbook contest in 1996 for his chapbook, *If I Could Imagine*. He won the 1997 Tennessee Middle State Chapbook contest with his chapbook *Among Men*. In 1999 the Laguna Poets Series published his fourth chapbook *Now She Bends Away* by Inevitable Press.

His poems "Among Men" and "Letters from Paul" were nominated for a Pushcart. He received an honorable mention for his poetry in The Chapel Jazz Poetry Contest in the spring of 1999, and he received an Excellence in Literature award from Mira Costa College.

He teaches English Composition, Literature and Creative Writing at National University in San Diego.

www.ingramcontent.com/pod-product-compliance
Lightning Source LLC
Chambersburg PA
CBHW031205090426
42736CB00009B/791